SHE RISES

steph nasou

SHE RISES
Copyright © 2022 by Stephanie Nasou
All rights reserved
Published by Red Penguin Books
Bellerose Village, New York
Library of Congress Control Number: 2022903517
ISBN
Print 978-1-63777-230-0 / 978-1-63777-231-7
Digital 978-1-63777-229-4
No part of this book may be reproduced in any form or by any electronic or mechanical means, including information storage and retrieval systems, without written permission from the author, except for the use of brief quotations in a book review.

steph nasou

These pieces are a direct reflection of going through the motions of the human condition. Learning about life and that death is a part of life. Going through hell just to find the light again. It is a compilation of healing, of life's ruptures and repairs.

dedicated to

Every person who has ever felt incredibly alone. You were always enough.

fall

photos by me

photo by Mary Anne Nason

my undoing

That's what I do.
I make things look prettier than they are.
I make myself look prettier than I am.
In reality, everything is blurry, without color, without intention.
Praise without actual admiration that I yearn for, from me, from you.
From anyone willing to give me the satisfaction of knowing- of being known.
I am losing the feeling of youth where those who worship the freeness of my being were unequivocally sullen by the factual rebuke of my flesh prison.
The way I wore my shirts, the way you wore your hats.
Your hair growing out from underneath like some adolescent eroticism. The highest degree of what you should have been.
What they expected you to be.
I love the expected, even though I spent my days purging in the unexpected.
Trying to unwind the meaning behind my fatality.
That I am too insignificant to understand.

In my way, I am singing a song of myself – a world unheard and a world unseen inside this body. The body that I try so hard to make look like other bodies.
Bodies of the beautiful, the sad and the free.
Bodies of those who do not waver in the contact of information – but digest the universe in separate swallows. Undoing their doings despite doing them again. Knowing that you're rotting, you're seething, you're yet again regretting that you can think without trying —
that all you can do is think and unravel what you've pretended to be.
In the bitterness of this world- unknowing, yet knowing that the fantasies are ever dying.
And I, in the fantasies, have never lived, in my own sudden skin- prosecuted by them- prosecuted by who I chose to live in those fantasies.

photo by me

mortality

Sometimes I pick apart the pieces of myself-
The words that fool my tongue roll sharply down.
I eat the poison I once picked in good health-
As I serenade your empty aisles.
When I follow a friend down a ravine-
I sent a spiral to my own God.
I ask if it were Winter in his machine.
I water castles of flowers you sent to me.
Tumbling down the rabbit hole-
I find myself crumbling like a piece of wheat bread.
Watching the white angels spread their discomfort among the trees.
"The fall was once a satin snow," the rabbit said.
He rents the license to the land-
And ate the apple from my hand.

youth-

it was cold then,
i was young.
all i could see was the church steeple and the roof beneath my feet.
it was crunching with the rustic orange of fall and i was falling
into a place i can't seem to find again
lost in a purgatory
waiting for a decision.
wish i could kiss your lungs,
wish i could heal your mind.

eyelits-

I am the movement through the trees, sporting their severed fingers,
Waving them like icicles.
Like inch-worms.
I'm crawling through the night—I have always seen you.
I am peeking through your basement window-- through the cellar,
Through your many doors.
I wait.
In your dreams, I speak to dead people
The dismembered bones of your past.
I will whisper illusions into your swollen edges.
Weaving them through each eyelet in my skin- I am round.
I'm waiting like the wolf.

photo by me.

-my love letter to the forest

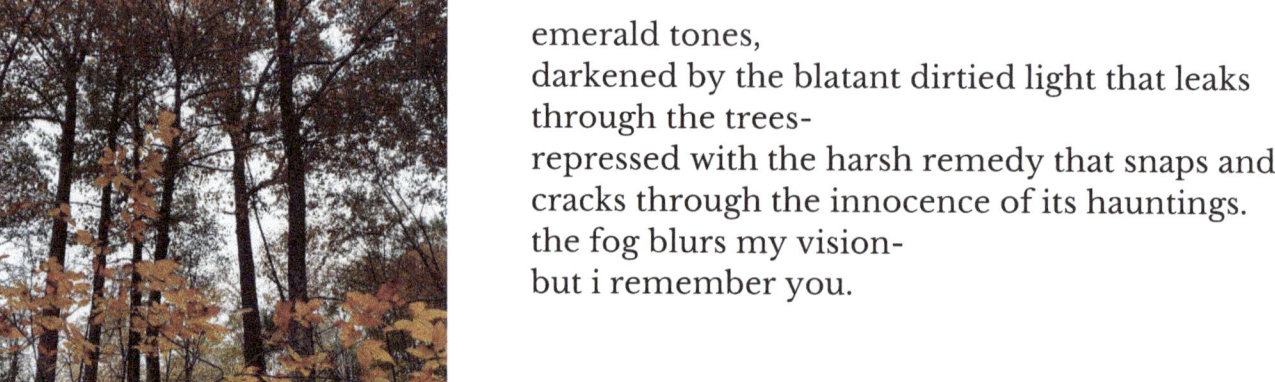

emerald tones,
darkened by the blatant dirtied light that leaks through the trees-
repressed with the harsh remedy that snaps and cracks through the innocence of its hauntings.
the fog blurs my vision-
but i remember you.

photo by Tim Jacobsen

my soul is a rainy night

my soul is a rainy night.
the windows tightly shut
like a fist
in my once
securely woven heart.
my soul is a rainy night.
where i rely on my own raindrops
to reveal my symptoms.
i am free of fear
i am free of the light.

photo by me

growing up

The light seeps in, it is all you know.
Softly seeking and guiding you to the places you must go,
Darkness is nothing but a shadow, cast on your future.

It will find you.

It soaks into you as if you already deserve it, only six years old and
you already need to serve it,
Your master.

We go through the motions of an everyday life and these thoughts
keep coming,
Even when we distract ourselves.

You're older now and have had children of your own
Born into a world you're unsure of
A ridiculous exposure to the bright light in front of them, pulling
them out of you into the villainous land you call your home.

Now they're talking about dates when you know you'll be dead.
Keeping on friendly terms with the person you used to be.
You've grown old now, but you can't feel your age like you felt your
first scraped knee.
You only feel like it like you felt your first
Bleeding heart.

Because soon it ends,
And now you go.

photo by me

winter

"it is winter again"

photo by Bridget Moynihan

It is Winter again. I see the snow fall through the calloused trees, like fingertips they dance across the promenade. I see him in his white t-shirt, his tie un-done like a child, his blue eyes reflecting the cold. A chill runs down my spine. "Did you try to die last night?" I ask him if he loves me and he nods. We both smell like cigarettes. We listen to that song he loves and I cry.
We dance all night. Our heads fill with ridiculous ideas. We'll never fall in love.

We drive into the night. We are kids.
His hands are tough. They contrast his eyes that try to be kind through the demon that possesses him. He wasn't always like this. He used to have dreams. He used to soar through the visions of a future, as if he had nothing to lose. Now his hands are around my neck. His eyes aren't kind. The powder has taken him away from me. He's done this before.
The Winter is over. The summer begins. I push aside the facts that he is hurting me. After all, the sun is shining in my eyes so bright, just like his did, before it took him. I pretend it isn't his fault. I lie.
I am consumed with the entity. I have become him, he has become me. I try to run, but my feet won't move. The ground is swallowing me. I'm used to feeling this way. He holds me in his hands like a doll. He pulls my puppet strings. I pull his.

At a party. I am there. Against the wall. He is pushing me. I see two people running up. My hair is pulled out into their hands. He is trying to convince me. He is trying to say anything but that he is sorry. They have saved me.
I am still here. I am still with him. He is looking at me for the answers. He is looking at me for the reason why. We are addicted.
I wean myself off him like a drug. We only see each other on weekends, but he still sleeps next to me. I am tired.
I sever the chord between us with a kitchen knife. I
stop looking at him. He stops looking at me.

The answers never come. We are two different people now.
I lift my eyes to the chapel across the street. I see the moon gleam through the starlight. The universe rides off with the memory, of a kid, or a devil, I used to know. My feet hit the snow, I am floating through an old consciousness. I remember him. It is Winter again.

self harm-

it was supposed to be
something for me.
you weren't supposed to know.

photo by me.

laughter—

he never brushed his teeth
we laughed
i wish i was laughing with him
but we didn't laugh.
or when we did it was fake.
i laughed because i loved him,
not because he was funny.

photo by me

the denial of abuse-

She threw knives at them.
I saw her in my shallow sleep.
I would lie awake, tears flooding my eyes.
Screaming.
Maybe she will come back.
Maybe he was her.
Her daughter lives with married men
This house he was born in, this house he will die in.
Where she hurt them.
Where she comes for me in my sleep.
Where she threw knives at them.

dreams-

Remember when we used to dream?
Instead of being comfortable.
Preparing ourselves by perfectly
spinning the tapestries of our lives into
an articulate sentence that rolls off our
tongues and into the existence of our
structures.
That crumble
and break
That keep us alive.
Isn't the mere thrill of it all to dream?
Even so that we never decide to

That we decide to hide our
hearts away from the heaviness
of simple burdens,
kept in secret corners where
the coroners of our minds
unravel our secrets
We are wasting our time
on the sullen, frigid truths we
are running from.

the end of the world-

These next poems are about two different kinds of the world ending. One is a movie-like scenario, where cars fall out of the sky and the moon crashes into the earth. The other is the end of the world we are forced to face on the inside- yet expected to quietly and respectfully continue on.

photos by me

the end of the world-

I waited every day for the world to end.
Waited in the mornings, in the evenings,
Even in the afternoons.
I was terrified of the inevitable.
I felt that a curse was on me
That I had grown tired of waiting for something so subliminal,
So extremely meaningless...
Until the day the world did end,
And much to my surprise I was not tense
Nor impatient
Nor screaming
Nor clawing away at my skin in the gradations I'd imagined
Like some kind of possession
Leaving my body behind
Soul breaching.
I did none of those things at all.

photos by Mary Anne Nason

I had felt pain,
In my head, in my chest, in every single cell of my peculiar body,
My auto-unique model.
I had felt pain- surging and creasing and squeezing through each vein like a black cancer,
Leaving my broken heart alive. Still beating
Still wondering when I would feel pain again.
I had felt pain,
In my head, in the impossible-to-see
In the place where I am alone
In the place where the pain is personified,
Trying desperately to push it away
Fighting, the end.

the end of the world part II-

photo by me

spring

photos by me

kids-

He surrounded you, like dogs on black leashes,
someone licking away the thought of
your lost innocence.
It was a changing of lights
He gave you a pill.
His face decorated with a colossal
vision beneath his glasses.
He was alien romping around a
summer club.
You were a sheep in a midst of the
monster.

photo by me

the smoke dances-

The smoke dances like my tortured ghosts across the flame.
They're taunting me,
But I am not sorry.
My doing is vast.
My intentions are stronger than your dark presence was in my life.
I find peace in myself
One day
I will
Find peace in myself.
And leave my ghosts behind,
that dance across the flame
that swallow my ambitions &
cut me down,
that vacuum my soul out from underneath me.
But their memory aches in my body,
their contentment pumps through my veins.

photos by me

someone else's fire-

photo by Mary Anne Nason

visions of you & her dance in my mind
am i as beautiful?
does my spine connect so gracefully to my bottom with the same spice and confidence that hers does?
can i ever compare to the magnificence
of someone that i hate?
i stop myself.
i am the spice.
who am i to compare myself to someone else's fire?

photos by me

their peak-

I walk through the giant doors that lead me to the end of an era. The end of my angst, my bullying, the nights I swore I'd never be able to show my face again. The way they taunted and tortured me like a flame.

They asked me to cut out my organs and let them feast upon them. Endings like these are the endings in which I should say "Bittersweet." But I cannot.

High school wasn't kind to me.

I'm leaving behind the soulless vultures who devoured my being. Who ate my soul and spit it out. I couldn't let them anymore. The teachers who scolded me for being myself- preaching my worth was at the end of their pencils. Grading my dignity as if it were their jobs to do so. Opening me up like a casket and watching my hurt pour out onto them. Choking on my yearning to no longer be a part of their society.

I'm walking through the stained glass now. Into my new eternity. I know it will be different this time. I am looking through the hidden door. The one I've been seeking. Their peak has ended,

i'm still alive.

photo by me.

safety-

I've never been here before
Carefully weaving a web of repair
Humans inevitably arguing
Word vomiting profanities
Apologizing after.
Regressing and repairing damage as nature does
Love spilling out
From every opening
Or closing
Inside of me.
I am whole.
I haven't known you always
But I'll know you until I go to the moon
& after
& after.

photos by Lukas Pestalozzi

summer

photo by me

photo by Mary Anne Nason

taking responsibility

Note to the reader: This short story is about someone I used to know. But in a way, it is about all of us. Everyone who has ever felt the incredible need to hide from their wrongdoings. This short story is about taking responsibility.

bed of nails-

Time stands still again and again for me. The smoke fills my lungs, I inhale, I exhale. I am alone in my silly, little world. The bags under my eyes grow increasingly greyer, although I use concealer to cover the damage I've done. If they see through me they will know my weakness.

I am hiding the damage done by my childhood. No one knows. Masking the invasions of truth that swallow me whole. I am 52 now. An age that has a family, a life of their own. I think I wanted that. I do not want to face myself.

I looked around last night at the mess I made. In my room. I saw all of the pieces of who I've been, scattered across my floor, infecting my loose consciousness that I show no one. I am clinging to a version of me that is stale. I no longer spend late nights dreaming of the future. I've willed that away.

I saw a glimpse of an old self. I was happy to see her. She was younger in her head, in her body. Her hair had never been touched by grey and her blue eyes never touched by disappointment in herself. I told her I was broken and she said she'd fix me. If I could go back. Could I? I'll dream tonight of an old world I once lived inside of. A world of 21. I will dream of myself. I will dream of yellow dresses and the full moon.

...

I closed my eyes and awoke. I felt well-rested, but somehow different. My body and mind were equals. I hadn't felt that in a long time. I opened my eyes to my old four walls and saw my BiC brass lighter in my hand. It was my favorite one. Lying on my bed, I looked ahead to find beads at my doorway. Where am I? I thought I was alone. Of course,... Cooper. My old boyfriend. My ex-husband. I saw him lying next to me. But wait- I remember this morning.

We had a dream last night. The hairs on our arms and our legs stood straight up. We were running through the forest on the forbidden taste of acid, rotting our brains. My head was whirling, but we were feeling fine. His fingertips were lava, his eyes were on fire. His hands stopped holding mine. We were in another universe.

I believed in other universes back then. We both did. Oh, how we were so very young. The days when we would run naked through the trees and visit every one of our demons, bark by bark. I saw him unwillingly change. I saw him stay the same.

bed of nails

I am awakened by my daydream still stuck in my adolescence. Cooper says I tried to jump off the roof last night. Silly, silly me. I was caught in a trip.

"Can I make my way back home?" I asked him, my eyes welling, my jaw clenching onto the words that tried to escape my mouth.

"Jan, baby, you are home," he said slowly. "What's the matter with you?"

"The matter with me? The matter with me is that I woke up 52 years old this morning and now I'm back in my college town, in my old room, with you! That's the problem with me," I said.

He lowered his eyes to mine. He laughed.

"Jan gotta stop doing that acid girl," he exclaimed with a howl, lighting up a bowl in the kitchen. He always used to light one up before his class. He couldn't bear to see his teachers sober. Not after what he did.

I stopped myself. Maybe I could enjoy myself here. I could see my old friends, I could go to the pub downtown. I could do everything I used to do. I sprang up from my old, sunken water bed and jolted towards my hanging beaded door.

"You know what, baby," I said with confidence, "I'm leaving you!"

I threw the beads to either side so oddly and frivolously. I was me again.

I ran down to the old town I used to call mine. I yelled at the top of my lungs. I was free. I saw the pub just north of Lockheart Street and the little hippie shop I used to spend all my money at when I lived just down the road.

My mother's voice popped up inside my head suddenly and disturbingly.

"Jan! You're going to be late for class again. Now this is not how you want to start off again. Gallivanting around like a juvenile delinquent."

"Mama?" I thought.

Mama had died a few years before. Well at least in the lifetime where I'm 52. She got real old and sick and I would visit her at her home. Which wasn't really a home at all, but a place she was forced to be. Mama didn't really mind all that much; She liked being taken care of.

After hearing her nagging yet comforting voice I thought one thing... I'm going to class.

I flung open the doors to my past concrete prison... school. And to my not-so surprise, I did not remember a damn thing. I never cared for school anyway. But maybe I should've. Maybe I should have paid more attention. Maybe this would be my second chance.

I had given up on my dreams to be a marine biologist when I was 28. I had just married Cooper and lost the baby. Cooper swore it was my alcohol problem, but I don't think I had one. After that I stayed away from everyone.

My relationship with Cooper disappeared like rain on the pavement. I blame him for most things. Hell, why wouldn't I? I would be floating in the middle of the ocean in my own marine biology research lab. I would have a career of my own if it wasn't for him. I would be happy. And I am not an alcoholic.

bed of nails-

I raised my hand in class. I told them what they wanted to hear. How did I know what to say? I never did. Why was everything working out for me today? I go back in time, just in time to get away from that piece of work of a husband, I go to class, I say all the right things.

Then an idea struck me. I'm getting out of this town. I'm going somewhere I've never been. I'm going to start over. Without Cooper, my life would have been great. It would have been filled with opportunity. I didn't deserve what happened to me. I'm starting a new life.

I popped up from my seat and ran out the door once again. Crazy how much running I was doing that day. How could I not? I had been blessed with another chance. A parallel universe opened like a 3-D saucer. I fell into the void. I was ready to start again.

I ran back to my old college apartment to collect my things. Cooper was still lying so smugly in my bed.

"Baby, baby where are you going?" Cooper said, with intent to weave me back into himself. He always had a way of loving that kept me coming back for more.

For a minute, I missed him. I shouldn't have left. I shared 15 years of marriage of him. He was a part of me. No, I needed to leave. This was all his fault.

"I'm going to do everything I wanted to do. I'm going to do everything I could have done if it weren't for you!" My yell pierced every atom in his body carrying an energy so stark that it would continue to exist among our two universes, as he would carry it with him until his body started to decay, in both.

I looked in my rear-view mirror and saw every ghost of my past, which didn't exist anymore. I had revoked their screams. Their severed tongues casting spells on me. Not anymore. I have finally escaped their crooked, rotten smiles. Those ghosts, tortured my very being. Taunted my memory, for decades.

Somehow the universe looked out for me. I relived the next 31 years all by myself. I became a marine biologist just as I had dreamt it. Now I sit by the bay every morning and enjoy my morning coffee. The birds sing a song that I won. Bees buzz around my head. The environment beams with excitement for my newfound life and the earth smiles at every sunset I created. I watch my children playing in the garden. They love nature too. They are the best kids I've ever known. My husband is very much better than Cooper, too. He listens. He says he will grow old and ugly with me. I go to fancy dinners every night and eat snails. It is really something special.

bed of nails-

    I re-wrote history. How could I be so clever? To travel through time. How interesting of the universe to present to me. Thank you.

    I close my eyes to go to sleep tonight. I am content in the perfect life I have made. The life I always wanted. I roll over to kiss my husband on the cheek.

    I shriek in disarray. It isn't my husband. I see the forest in his eyes, the void is swallowing me. This can't be happening. I am falling back into myself. I am falling back onto their bed of nails.

    I wake up in the same old dump I'd been living in for 15 years, surrounded by the ~~mess~~ I had made. In my room.

special thanks to

Everyone who has stood by my side, believed in my work and loved me through it all.

My parents Peter and Mary Anne Nasou.

Mary Anne Nasou, Bridget Moynihan, Andrew Smith, Lukas Pestalozzi, Tim Jacobsen and Matthew Dees for their excellent photography. Thank you for supporting my visions and making them a reality with me. I could not have compiled this without you.

www.ingramcontent.com/pod-product-compliance
Lightning Source LLC
Chambersburg PA
CBHW061114070526
44583CB00027B/3287